CW00663902

Very kindly
Donated
by
Mrs. Honham
Summer 2019

15220

Photographs © Ted Scott, 2013

Text © Heritage Publishing Ltd, 2013

Typographical design © David Bateman Ltd, 2013

Published in 2013 by David Bateman Ltd

30 Tarndale Grove, Albany, Auckland, New Zealand

Reprinted 2015, 2018

www.batemanpublishing.co.nz

ISBN 978-1-86953-851-4

Book design: Catherine Wells, Heritage Publishing Ltd

Photographs: Ted Scott, Fotofile Ltd

Printed in China by Everbest Printing Company

Previous Page: Northland. Tapotupotu Bay

Contents

Introduction

This book represents a journey from Cape Reinga in the north to Fiordland, situated at the far south-west corner of the South Island. New Zealand is a long, narrow country (1,600 kilometres long by 400 kilometres at widest point), separated into two main islands by the Cook Strait.

The North Island has a more temperate climate while the South Island experiences colder winters. However, what both islands share is a landscape of rugged and awe-inspiring proportions shaped by the tectonic plates on which the country sits. The evidence of this upheaval is in the volcanoes and thermal region of the North Island, while the plate movement has created the spectacular Southern Alps of the South Island. The landscape is under continual transformation from volcanoes, earthquakes, gale force winds, and rain. Its 15,000 kilometres of coastline is constantly battered by the relentless surf of the Pacific Ocean along the east coast and the Tasman Sea along the west. More tranquil waters in the Bay of Islands, in the north and the Marlborough Sounds at the top of the South Island are favoured by yachtsmen. Empty beaches abound, from the white sands of the east coast to the black iron sands of Auckland's west coast. Although the original forest cover, which stretched from shore to shore, has been reduced by land clearance for farming, vast areas of forest remain. These forests dominate the west and south-west of the South Island. To this day, large areas of Fiordland remain unexplored.

Most of the images for this book were taken at locations accessible to all travellers. Even the aerial photos were taken using local tourist flight operators. We have also included location maps with page markers on pages 126 and 127 so that fellow travellers can find and experience the same view.

Explore and enjoy.

Ted Scott, Karekare 2013

Opposite: West Coast. Coastline, Kahurangi National Park
Next page: Great Barrier Island. Entrance to Fitzroy Harbour

Northland

Cape Reinga
Opposite: Cape Reinga Lighthouse

Subtropical Northland is rich in culture and history, as well as natural beauty. The sheltered and picturesque Bay of Islands is a stunning contrast to the stark beauty of the often wind-swept western coastline. Cape Reinga, where the Tasman Sea meets the Pacific, is sacred to Maori as the place where the spirits of the departed descend to the underworld to return to their traditional Hawaiki homeland. The region is overseen by the iconic Tane Mahuta, New Zealand's biggest tree, standing in Waipoua Forest as a reminder of the kauri forests that once clothed vast tracts of the peninsula.

Spirits Bay

Whangaroa Harbour

Historic Northland churches
1 Hikurangi to Kawakawa Road. Old Chapel
2 Waimate North, St John the Baptist Church
3 Hokianga. Mangungu Mission Chapel, Horeke
4 Matakohe. Window detail
5 Te Kao. Ratana Church
6 Matakohe. Coates Memorial Church

Kaipara. Minniesdale Chapel, Wharehine

Hokianga Harbour entrance

Henderson Bay
Next page: Parengarenga Harbour. Silica sands

Northland evening
Opposite: Waipoua Forest. Home of Tane Mahuta, the ancient giant kauri tree

North Auckland
1 Puhoi River kayaking
2 Riverhead excursion boat
3 Tawharanui Regional Park
4 Sandspit. Fishermen
5 Muriwai. The Flat Rock

Kawau Island. Mansion House Bay

21

Auckland

Auckland City. Classic Yacht, Waitemata Harbour
Opposite: West Auckland. Lion Rock, Piha

With Auckland City 'Tamaki Makau Rau' situated on a narrow isthmus between the Waitemata and Manukau Harbours, nowhere is far from the sea. So it is easy to understand why there are more yachts and launches per capita here than anywhere else in the world, earning Auckland the title of 'City of Sails'. The sheltered bays and many islands of the Hauraki Gulf provide an ideal playground for Aucklanders. Back on shore, much of the metropolitan area of New Zealand's commercial hub and largest city is nestled around the 50 cones of the Auckland volcanic field. To the west, rain forest blankets the Waitakere Ranges and provides a stunning backdrop to the world-famous surf beaches of Piha, Karekare and Muriwai.

1 Mission Bay. View to Rangitoto Island
2 Waiheke Island. Stony Batter
3 Waitemata Harbour. Racing
4 Hauraki Gulf. Little Barrier Island

5 Hauraki Gulf. Pakatoa Island
6 Harbour Bridge. Dawn
Opposite: Auckland. View northeast over CBD
Next page: Auckland. View northwest above Albert Park

West Auckland. Reflections, Whatipu

West Auckland
1 Waitakere Ranges. Stream
2 Piha. Annual surf boat races
3 Bethells Beach. Surf watch tower
4 Muriwai. Gannet colony
5 Karekare Beach. The Watchman

Manukau Harbour. South Head
Opposite: Waitakere Ranges. Pohutukawa amongst white-flowering manuka

Waikato

Miranda. Sunflower crop
Opposite: Waikato River

The Waikato River, New Zealand's longest, flows from the slopes of Mt Ruapehu, through Lake Taupo and the fertile Waikato Plains to the Tasman Sea. It gives the Waikato region not just its name, but defines the landscape and economy with the fertile soils underpinning the region's extensive farmlands. By contrast, the bush-covered Coromandel Peninsula to the north is a popular holiday destination with pristine beaches, sheltered harbours and breathtaking views.

1 Thames. Tapu Water Gardens
2 Whitianga
3 Cathedral Cove
4 Ngaruawahia. Waka
5 Kuaotunu Beach
6 Mercury Bay
Opposite: Raglan. Bridal Veil Falls

Central Plateau and Thermal Region

View south: Blue Lake, Mount Tongariro, Mount Ngauruhoe and snow covered Mount Ruapehu
Opposite: View north: Upper and Lower Tama Lakes and Mount Ngauruhoe
Next page: Rotorua. Pohutu Geyser

This extensive geothermal area runs from the volcanoes of the central North Island through Rotorua to New Zealand's most active volcano, the Bay of Plenty's White Island. The volcanic cones of Tongariro, Ngauruhoe and Ruapehu, forming the basis of Tongariro National Park, were gifted to the Crown by Ngati Tuwharetoa, and being given dual World Heritage status recognises both their natural and cultural significance. The region is a tourist drawcard with winter skiing, the world-famous Tongariro Crossing walk, geysers and mud pools of Rotorua, and the sun-soaked beaches of the Bay of Plenty.

Rotorua. Bowls, Government Gardens and historic Bath House Museum

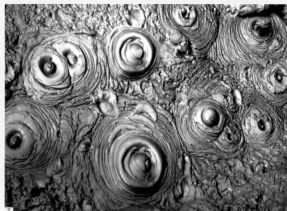

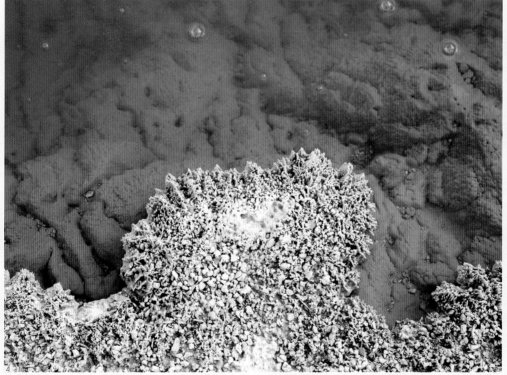

Thermal area

1 Rotorua. Modern Maori
carving
2 Ohinemutu. Stained-
glass window, Tama-te-
kapua meeting house
3 Rotorua. Boiling mud
pool, Whakarewarewa
4 Waiotapu geothermal
area. Champagne Pool
5 Rotorua. Memorial
gateway detail,
Whakarewarewa

Lake Taupo

Mount Ruapehu. Major eruption 1996

Taranaki

Lake Mangamahoe.
Opposite: Mount Taranaki

The spectacular Mount Taranaki 'shining peak' dominates the local landscape. According to Maori mythology Taranaki once lived with the other great volcanoes, Tongariro, Ruapehu and Ngauruhoe, but he was banished after falling in love with Tongariro's wife and headed west, carving out the Whanganui River as he went. The area around the city of New Plymouth is well-known for its black sand surf beaches and the beautiful rhododendron gardens of Pukeiti, Hollard Gardens, Pukekura Park and Tupare. The rich volcanic soils of Taranaki mainly support dairy farming, but sheep farming is more dominant in the neighbouring Manawatu district.

Tongaporutu. Coastal rock formations that are constantly being eroded by the Tasman Sea

Mount Taranaki dominates the Inglewood Golf Course

East Cape and Hawke's Bay

East Cape. Coastline

The remote rural East Coast with its strong Maori culture is the first place to be touched by the new dawn each day. Further south, the long, hot summers and cool winters of Hawke's Bay provide perfect conditions for growing grapes, and the whole area is renowned for its horticulture and viticulture. The region has long been known as the 'Fruit Bowl of New Zealand', and has many large orchards and over 70 vineyards peppering the landscape. Napier's title of 'the Art Deco City' stems from its reconstruction in the 1930s following a massive earthquake, and it is now a living tribute to the styles of that period.

Tolaga Bay
Next page: Hawke's Bay. Te Mata Peak

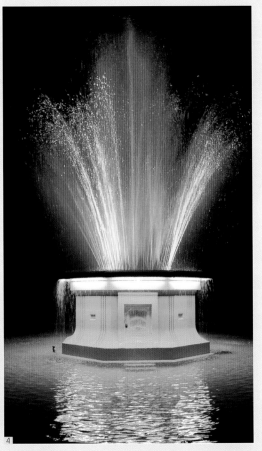

Napier
1 Art Deco building
2 1914 – 1918 War Memorial
3 Art Deco doorway
4 Tom Parker Fountain
5 Esplanade

Hastings. Te Mata Estate vineyard

Wellington

Civic Square. Sculpture
Opposite: The Beehive, part of New Zealand's Parliament Buildings

At the southern tip of the North Island adjacent to Cook Strait, lies the capital city, Wellington, and its harbour. A compact and vibrant city, its buildings cling precariously to steep hillsides and a rugged coastline. Dominating the art-lined city waterfront is the bold and innovative national museum, The Museum of New Zealand Te Papa Tongarewa.

Oriental Bay. Hillside dwellings

Mount Victoria. View west to central Wellington

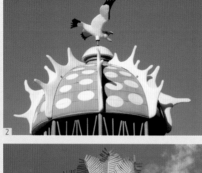

Wellington central city
1 City to Sea Bridge, Civic Square
2 Waterfront playground detail
3 Nikau Palms, Civic Square
4 *Solace in the Wind*, waterfront
5 Kupe Statue, waterfront
6 Fern Ball, Civic Square

Museum of New Zealand Te Papa Tongarewa

Nelson and Tasman

Farewell Spit
Opposite: Golden Bay

Situated in the north-west of the South Island, the Nelson and Tasman regions are known for year-round sunshine and three magnificent national parks. Abel Tasman National Park is a coastal wonderland with golden beaches; Nelson Lakes National Park comprises tranquil beech forest, craggy mountains and brooding lakes, while Kahurangi, New Zealand's second-largest national park, contains some of the world's deepest caves in its remote wilderness. Over the windy Takaka Hill from Nelson is Golden Bay, dubbed New Zealand's 'best-kept secret', and treasured for its laid-back lifestyle and creative community of working artists. The remote and beautiful Farewell Spit lies at the end of the road through Golden Bay.

Tasman. Old farm building, Wakefield

1 Tasman. Lake Rotoiti, Nelson Lakes National Park
2 Nelson. Sailing dinghies
3 Nelson. Christ Church Cathedral
4 Tasman. Wharariki Beach
5 Nelson. Tahunanui Beach
6 Abel Tasman National Park
7 Abel Tasman National Park. Falls River
Next page: Tasman. Entrance to the Whanganui Inlet

Abel Tasman National Park

Nelson. Cable Bay sunset

Marlborough and Kaikoura

Marlborough. Brancott Estate
Opposite: Kaikoura. Pohutukawa

Just across Cook Strait from Wellington, the Marlborough Sounds are home to all kinds of bird and sea life, including little blue penguins, dolphins and seals. Just to the south, the Marlborough region regularly records the highest sunshine hours in New Zealand. No surprise then that this is the country's number one grape-growing and wine-making region, widely considered by critics to produce some of the world's best Sauvignon Blanc. A little further down State Highway One is Kaikoura's stunning coastal and alpine beauty. The mountains rise almost directly out of the ocean in places, and with the deep Hikurangi Trench lying very close to shore, Kaikoura is one of the planet's top whale-watching spots.

Kaikoura. Evening

1 Picton. Waterfront
2 Marlborough Sounds. Governors Bay
3 Marlborough Sounds. Waiting for the ferry
4 Marlborough. Landscape
5 Picton. Marina
6 Marlborough. Pelorus Bridge
7 Marlborough. Lake Grassmere

Kaikoura. Lavender farm

Kaikoura. Seals with pups
Next page: Kaikoura Ranges

Canterbury and Mackenzie Basin

Christchurch. Peacock Fountain
Opposite: Christchurch. Port Hills

The vast and varied Canterbury region stretches from the Pacific Ocean across the fertile Canterbury Plains to the snow-capped peaks of the Southern Alps. The region's main city, Christchurch, is steadily rebuilding itself after the earthquakes of 2010 and 2011. East of Christchurch are Lyttelton Harbour, Banks Peninsula and the picturesque harbour-side village of Akaroa. To the south-west the stark tussock-covered Mackenzie Basin is a landscape of imposing glacial lakes and dramatic mountain peaks. It is the gateway to the Mount Cook National Park and home to one of the world's few dark sky reserves at Tekapo.

Banks Peninsula. Akaroa Harbour

Mackenzie Basin. Lake Pukaki

High-country farming
1 Albury. Moving cattle
2 Tekapo. Sheep
3 Aoraki, Mount Cook

North Canterbury. Ferniehurst

Lindis Pass, linking Mackenzie Basin with Otago

Mackenzie Basin. Looking north-west towards the Gamack Range and Southern Alps

Mount Dobson. Burkes Pass, gateway to the Mackenzie Basin

Mackenzie Basin. Tekapo Canal
Next page: Lake Pukaki and Aoraki/Mount Cook

Mackenzie Basin. Lake Tekapo

Canterbury and Mackenzie Basin
1 Mount John Observatory, Lake Alexandrina beyond
2 Lyttelton Harbour. Governors Bay Wharf
3 Timaru. Street art
4 Timaru. Sculpture of the famous racehorse Phar Lap
5 Tekapo. Mackenzie's Dog
6 Lake Tekapo. Silhouettes

Otago and Southland

Otago. Kakanui Mountains near Ranfurly
Opposite: Otago. Confluence of the Clutha and Cardrona Rivers, Albert Town

The varied Otago region extends down the coast from the whitestone heritage buildings of Oamaru, past the Waitaki River and huge spherical boulders strewn in the sand at Moeraki, to Dunedin – New Zealand's oldest city founded by Scottish settlers and goldminers over 150 years ago. Inland, via the dramatic open landscapes of Central Otago, lies the winter sports and adventure capital of Queenstown. The lush, green pastoral farmlands of Southland form a marked contrast to the dryness of inland Otago.

Central Otago. Lake Wakatipu, *SS Earnslaw*

Central Otago. Queenstown

Otago Winter Playground
1 Treble Cone. Parasail
2 Dart River. Jet boat
3 Cardrona Ski-field

4 Lake Wakatipu. Glenorchy Jetty
5 Lake Wakatipu. Glenorchy ice wall
Opposite: Lake Wanaka

Otago. Hills near Fairlight

Central Otago. Lake Hawea
Next page: Central Otago, St Bathans. The Blue Lake, Goldfields Park

Otago. Karitane, Waikouaiti River mouth

Otago. Moeraki boulders

Southland. Blue Cliffs Beach

Historic Buildings

1 Dunedin. Allied Press Building
2 Dunedin. Terrace houses
3 Dunedin. Otago University
4 Ranfurly. Milk bar
5 Oamaru. Colonial buildings
6 Dunedin. Larnach Castle
7 St Bathans. Vulcan Hotel
8 Arrowtown. Historic cottages
9 Southland. Waipapa Point
  lighthouse

Fiordland

Sutherland Sound

The dramatic and jaw-dropping natural beauty of Fiordland has earned it World Heritage status and explains why it is known as the 'sightseeing and walking capital of the world'. The vast Fiordland National Park dominates the region, showcasing dramatic wilderness on a grand scale. Waterfalls tumble hundreds of metres into pristine, forested valleys and deep, sheer sided fiords carved during past ice ages reach, finger-like, towards the wild Tasman Sea.

Milford Sound. Mitre Peak shrouded in cloud

Fiordland. Te Anau

Fiordland. Murchison Mountains

Fiordland. Hollyford River
Opposite: Milford Track. Sutherland Falls

West Coast

Lake Matheson
Previous Page: West Coast. Fox River

Gold enticed fortune-seekers here in the early days, followed soon after by coal. Today the West Coast is best known as a natural wonderland, with its rivers and rainforests, lakes and lagoons, glaciers and geological treasures, as well as pounamu, the sacred greenstone found only in this region, which Maori traded across the country. Included with Fiordland in the Te Wāhipounamu World Heritage area of south-west New Zealand are the Fox and Franz Josef glaciers. In the north the Heaphy Track, the longest of New Zealand's Great Walks, connects the West Coast to Golden Bay.

Southern Alps. View over the Fox Range showing Aoraki/Mount Cook National Park,

West Coast beech forest
Opposite: Haast Pass. Fantail Falls

Lake Matheson. Forest glade

Franz Josef Glacier

Punakaiki. Blowhole at Pancake Rocks

Westport. Buller River anchorage

Carters Beach, south of Westport

Cape Foulwind. Seal Colony
Next page: Franz Josef. Waiho River

Southern Alps. Mt Sefton
West Coast. Forest with red-flowering Southern Rata

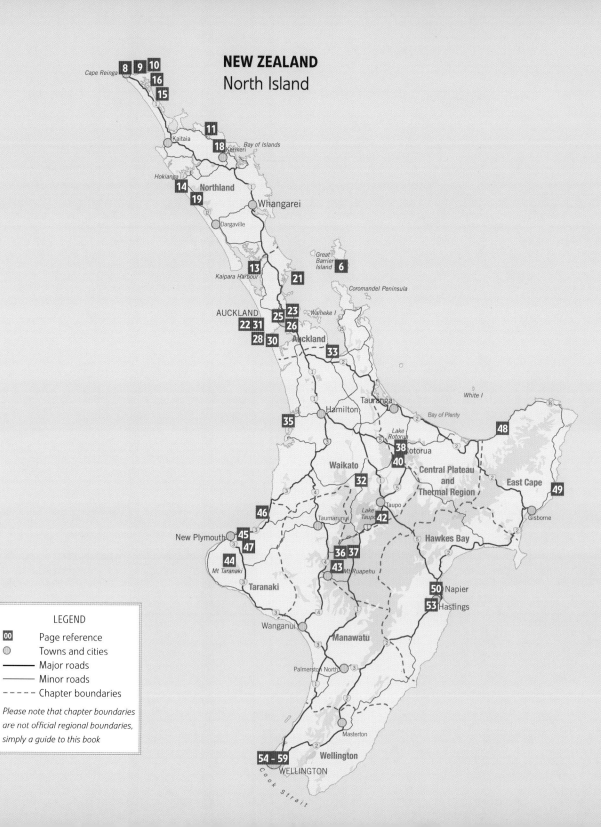

NEW ZEALAND
North Island

LEGEND

00 Page reference

● Towns and cities

━━ Major roads

── Minor roads

┈┈ Chapter boundaries

*Please note that chapter boundaries
are not official regional boundaries,
simply a guide to this book*

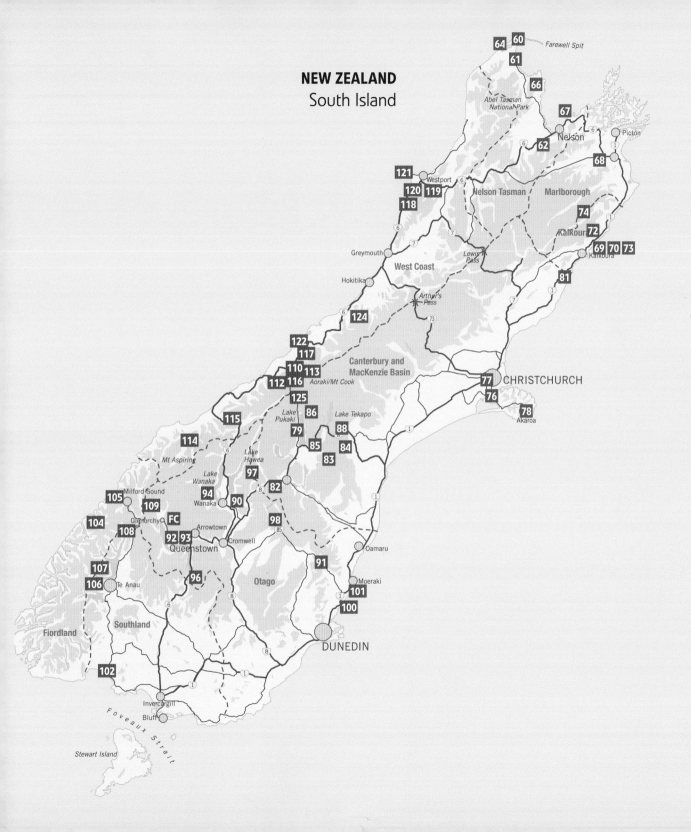

NEW ZEALAND
South Island

64 60 *Farewell Spit*

61

66

Abel Tasman National Park

67

62 Nelson

6

6

Picton

121 Westport

68

120 119 Nelson Tasman Marlborough

118

6

74

Greymouth 7 72

Kaikoura

West Coast *Lewis Pass* 69 70 73

Hokitika Kaikoura

Arthur's Pass 7

81

124 73 1

122

117 Canterbury and MacKenzie Basin

110 113

112 116 *Aoraki/Mt Cook* 77 CHRISTCHURCH

125 76

Lake Pukaki 86 *Lake Tekapo* 78

115 79 Akaroa

114 85 88

Mt Aspiring *Lake Hawea* 84

97 83

Lake Wanaka 82 1

105 Milford Sound 94

109 Wanaka 90

104 98

108 Glenorchy FC

Arrowtown 85

92 93 Cromwell

Queenstown Oamaru

91

107 Otago

106 Te Anau 96 Moeraki

101

100

Fiordland Southland 6 8

8 DUNEDIN

8

102

1 Invercargill

Bluff

F o v e a u x   S t r a i t

Stewart Island